LIMERICKS OF DEATH

By Sean Seville

POETRY INDEX

INTRODUCTION

Contrary to what a limerick is, each of these poems are much longer than five lines. Twisted humor is consistent within every one of them. Violence begets violence. Death plays a key part in life- the end. The recurring theme throughout this publication is death, in its most horrid, volatile, despicable, and morbid form.

Life is beautiful and precious to those that make the most of it. What about death? Is it nothing more than a dismal finale to the joy that life brings us? Death can be beautiful as well. Perhaps it can be used as a way for pain and suffering to cease.

The day will come when you are laid out on a cold steel table, and a coroner will examine your lifeless corpse. Your temple of flesh that was once so precious to you will be nothing more than a hollow vessel. Maybe that's not a beautiful notion, but depending on the kind of life one lives, death might be the only catharsis to experience If that is the case for any individual, they must have lived an abysmal life indeed. This would be a circumstance in which death is truly a gift.

Can you hear the howling of the wind? Can you feel it pierce your soul with its cold artic blast? The Grim Reaper will traverse this realm coming ever so closer to taking someone you know, love, or even you back with him to the farthest regions of the netherworld. Can you see the eternal suffering of those sentenced to damnation in various bolgias of the nine circles of Hell? Is there a Heaven?

I only hear the cries of despair in an infinite hailstorm of fire and brimstone. Screams are reciprocated with laughter. precipitation of ashes shall fall from the crimson sky. The freaks who dwell in my presence, taunting me with kerosene and matches know no ill except in their own minds.

My lady, may I have this dance, for this is the dance of death?! These are just a few of my happy thoughts. Just kidding... half kidding, anyway. Now let the bliss of malevolence in the form of poetry commence!

8

8

ODE TO THE AXE MURDERER

Out of my restraints I almost swooned,
The rope burn hurts this is no cartoon
Over the hills and through the woods
I'd scream for help if I could
The sealant has dried that covers my mouth
I huff and puff and simply pout
Must flee on foot to escape
a most heinous indescribable fate
A ruptured spleen and a broken pelvis
he's after me heaven help us
I hide behind trees no time to relax
He's stark raving mad holding an axe
Poor Lucinda she begged and begged
The son of a bitch still chopped off her legs
What were you thinking, drinking, and spill
a glass of scotch with a roofie pill
The assailant has date rape on his mind
Thoughts of tying her up so sublime
She broke a nail, he broke her nose
This is the life that we chose I suppose
More cocaine up in her nose,
Watch as the blood steadily flows

The court must condemn and execute
The devious, murderous, fiendish brute
I asked the police to search his cellar
Please listen to me, why won't you help her?
He's a rapist, a drunk, and a maniac,
a sadistic lunatic in fact
I barely got away from him,
The bringer of death, a man so grim
Fa la la, I see I saw
He grabbed a hacksaw, amputated her arms
He won't stay away he'll murder and maim
Next victim will come and he'll do the same
Practice makes perfect for a malevolent soul
He flushed the girl's heart down the tidy bowl
All her remains are in the basement
Stacked up in crates an improper placement
A stillborn fetus cut from the belly
The man ate its brains with p.b. and jelly
The baby's legs covered in eggs
Its tiny nips smothered in grits
Quite a feast fit for a king
Nothing is quite what it seems
This is a disaster, I demand answers
A philanthropist that smells like fish
I returned to his home and that's a fact
No evidence, no clues, no bloody axe

Chloroform in my nostrils, I blacked out
When I regained consciousness I started to shout
The killer laughed as he tied me up
He caressed my hair, his sweet buttercup
Should have gone away when I still had the chance
I was so scared I pissed in my pants
It was pointless to plead, and beg as I dread
The psychopath swung his axe and chopped off my head

COOKING WITH ISABELLE

The corpse slowly rots all matter decays
As the body decomposes her shadow remains
Hush now sweet Isabelle tongue in cheek
I threw her into a ditch so deep
The voices in my head won't leave me alone
They ordered me to cut her down to the bone
My senses are shot my vision is blurry
Must cover the burial plot in a hurry
I always see Isabelle she's in my dreams
I burned off her flesh with simmering hot steam
No reason to fear, fret not my love
You're now a golden winged angel in heaven above
Or a mangy dog that dwells in hell
I impaled her with a pitchfork when she fell
Cut out her tongue and remove the breasts
This pair is more tender than the rest
Fricassee the food and pour on some gravy
The correct seasoning make them so savory
Filet of fingers seal the deal
Spaghetti and eyeballs a delicious meal
There's nothing like an internal organ buffet
A quiet dinner for two, what do you say?
The voices had warned me, it was foreseen
I served Isabelle's ovaries and licked my plate clean

13

ASPIRATIONS OF AN ARSONIST

Fire, fire flames so bright
First house I set on fire tonight
I have sealed your fate/You will meet your doom
You have never met anyone quite like this loon
I like to play with matches/God, tell me why?
Black ashes are falling from the sky
A woman wore a black evening gown/
She looked so pristine
Barricade the bathroom door/I heard the screams
Such a sassy broad, but a delicate dame
Her body was consumed and ravaged by flames
Must get away/Out of mind, out of sight
I have many more frivolous fires to ignite
Do not mope, cannot cope with lacking such hope
Don't want to be lynched, dancing at the end of a rope
I'll make sure you suffer first degree burns
Empty extinguisher? You'll never learn
Think you will get the best of me, don't make me laugh
Better make an appointment for another skin graft
Try not to be bashful, shy, or meek
Just because we make fun of a disfigured freak
You weren't exactly easy on the eyes from the start

15

Now they'll push you around in a shopping cart
Peeled crispy skin and faltering flesh
Plead for your life/that will cause you distress
Poured gasoline from a canister in the daughter's bedroom
Do you miss your dead mommy?/You'll see her soon
I'll strike a match and you make a wish
I hear a fire engine's siren/Something's amiss
The father had died from asphyxiation
Same fate for the girl caused by smoke inhalation
I vacated the premises/
Escaped through the kitchen back door
Wait till you see what I have in store
Turned on the stove so gas fills the room
Watch with high expectations as the house goes "ka-boom"
Eagerly observed from the down the street
Firemen entered the homestead/My heart skipped a beat
Things could have gone differently/
Remorse, there was none
The explosion blew everyone to Kingdom Come

THE DEVIL MADE ME DO IT

Woke up this morning with blood in my eye
My agenda is murder/Who's turn to die?
Check your box of cracker jacks for a surprise
Max turned his back on me/That wasn't wise
I slit his throat with a butcher knife
Hope he had life insurance for his widowed wife
Hardy, har, har, she didn't get far
Her mutilated corpse in the trunk of my car
Sonya's blood was spattered on the dashboard
A fitting fate for such a young whore
All promiscuous women should be destroyed
The victim tried to escape and I became annoyed
Doctor, I'm sick and there is no remedy
Police patrol cars are within the vicinity
Here is a thought that's straight from the heart
Dismember her body and spread it apart
Get a shovel and dig a hole until the break of dawn
Or cremate her remains/Sprinkle them out on the lawn
Send the devil a soul, or two, or five
Massacre them all/No one is to survive
My identity is unknown/My soul is at stake
Sonya's dead body at the bottom of a lake

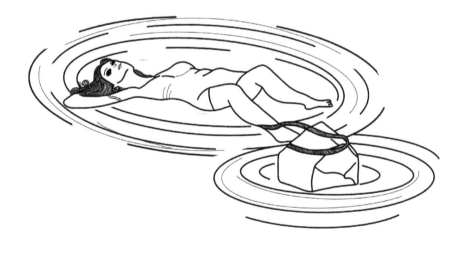

Love to go see her/I'd have to go swimming
Can't spare the time, too busy sinning
Lord be thy shepherd/Wrangle thou sheep
Dug out Sonya's eyes with a switchblade/
A just cause to weep
How much more of this blood will spill?
Gallons will be lost as I have the will
Satan, tell me how many more lives must I take?
If I go to prison there is no escape
Max's bloody torso on the porch was a mess
The police had restrained me/I was under arrest

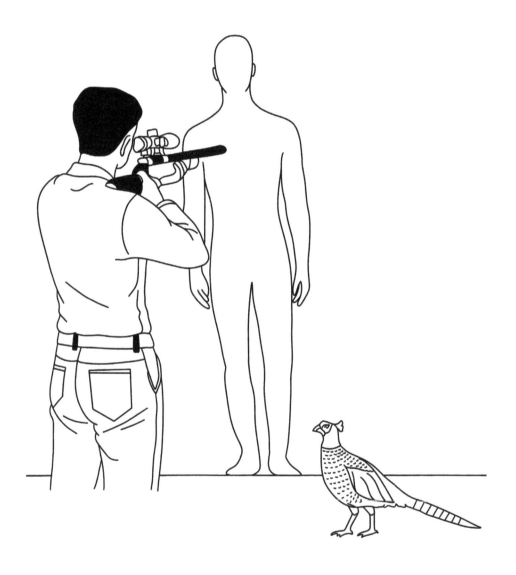

HUNTING FOR AN IDENTITY

Ralphie was eager to go hunting in the woods
He was determined to bring home a deer if he could
His friends Paul and Winston accompanied
him for the ride
This was nothing short of suicide
Ralphie was of the demented sort
Attempting to kill animals is a plan to abort
Both Paul and Winston were a couple of cynics
They were fully aware that Ralphie was schizophrenic
Why would he want to take his two friends for a ride?
Ralphie surmised that both men were eager to die
As far as he was concerned there was nothing
wrong with his mentality
A former vice president was a split personality
Winston and Paul often addressed their friend as
"Dick Cheney"
They got scared and jumped out of the moving car/
It began raining
Ralphie wanted to shoot pheasants/
That's what he would say
But he'd rather hunt man/His friends were the prey
Paul and Winston ran away/

Ralph followed their tracks
He had Paul in the sight of his rifle,
and shot him in the back
Dick Cheney, Dick Cheney a tyrant at will
Dick Cheney, Dick Cheney with a heart made of steel
He was always Hell bent on world domination
For all he's done for this country he deserved a vacation
Dick said, "I'm sorry. Believe me, it was not my fault
It was not my intention for you to get caught
In the sight of my rifle/I told you to run
I hold in my hands a pretty big gun
It has an infrared beam/Guess you didn't see the dot
Who told you to walk directly in front of my shot?"
Cheney was concerned for his friend, and prayed
he wasn't dead
He pulled the trigger of his rifle, and put a
bullet in Paul's head
Dick Cheney, Dick Cheney hunted ducks and quail
Dick Cheney, Dick Cheney sent Paul straight to hell
Winston couldn't believe the level of his plight
He diligently trekked through the fortuitous night
Cheney discovered his target hiding by a tree
Winston hastily dropped down to his knees
The "ex-vice president" aimed the gun at his
friend's abdomen instead of his head
Without a moment's hesitation he proudly said,

"It wasn't Bush's administration/
Who do you think really called the shots?
The so called 'war on terror' was my devious plot
You pissed yourself like a girl/Perhaps you should douche
It was all your fault/Should have never voted for Bush"
The recession has been hard on everyone/
Who can you trust?
Cheney pulled the trigger of his rifle and
spilled Winston's guts

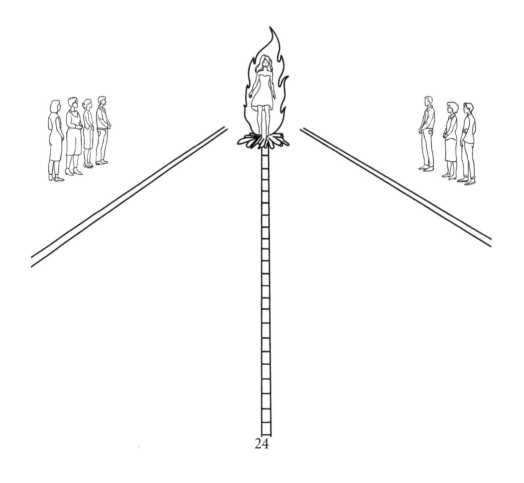

24

TRAGEDY ON THE CATWALK

Molly McDermott was a glamorous model
who enjoyed her work
Receiving free designer clothes was her favorite perk
Jasmine felt for Molly nothing but contempt
Which model did she hate the most? Here is a little hint:
She imagined Molly tied up, burning at the stake
Proper retribution for a witch/Oh, for goodness sake
She thought, "I should be in the limelight/
It's my turn to shine
All of her contracts and the sponsors,
 endorsements shall be mine
She and I will model at a show tonight/
What tremendous luck
Dan will strangulate Molly at a farm,
and ditch her corpse in the muck
The time has come for Molly to do h
er little turn on the catwalk
I'll split your head wide open and
have you outlined in chalk
Tell her to break a leg/If she doesn't I'll break it for her
Then I'd have to go and spend
good money on a defense lawyer

Molly knows the routine all too well/
There is no need to be concerned
She'll go out and strut her stuff/
Walk, lean, twist, turn
Even without makeup McDermott looks amazing
You can do what you do best, bitch/
I'll be backstage waiting
I could strip you naked, stab your chest,
you should use your bra for a tourniquet
Slap you silly, snap your chicken neck/
That's the best way for me to handle it."
It should not come as a shock to learn
that Jasmine was envious/No happiness or bliss
I can give you the details of molly's fate if you insist
Molly glided down the catwalk with
elegance and such grace
Jasmine doused McDermott with
sulfuric acid in the face
The paparazzi snapped photographs of
Molly as she screamed
Jasmine struggled not to laugh because
that's just plain mean
She said, "You're no longer a beauty/
Now you hit an all time low
Haven't you heard the old cliché,
that you'll reap what you sow?"

Will Molly ever recover?/We may never know
Jasmine pranced around with
Dan merrily dancing/Do si do
That night Molly was in a hospital bed
hooked up to a respirator
Jasmine visited her with much delight/
She said, "See you later, alligator."
The jealous woman began to stomp
her feet as if she saw a bug
Then she leaned over molly's bed and
quickly pulled the plug

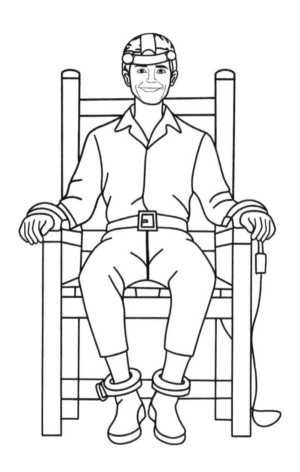

HOORAY FOR THE DEATH PENALTY

Seth Lundren has been on death
row for nearly fifteen years
His attorney can no longer file appeals/Oh, dear
Lundren is masochistic and has no fear
He was overcome with joy, now that the end is near
The man used to get pleasure derived from pain
Inserting needles into his testicles/
getting whipped with a chain
Shoving his hand down in the kitchen sink drain,
with no reason to linger
Turned on the garbage disposal and
lost a couple of fingers
Often late at night he fantasized of his wife
Bludgeoning her with a golf club/taking her life
Dissected the woman while using a hunting knife
Recollection of living a life of strife
Many people found the prospect of execution, terrifying
But Lundren couldn't wait to go and ride the lightning
Seth made a request for his last supper
Potatoes au gratin/He hoped there was enough of
The macaroni and scallops, lobster and steak
Lundren was going to the chair with a tummy ache

Seth had grown fond of prison life,
and wished that he could stay
The barber arrived at his cell/
Lundren was going to get his head shaved
After the haircut a priest came and offered a prayer
Lundren attacked him and an officer
stunned Seth with a taser
Later in preparation for the main event
officers ordered Seth to drop his pants
Lundren became giddy, smiled with glee and said,
"Hot damn"
An officer shoved some cotton inside
the confines of Seth's anus
Then was fitted with a diaper/
put in restraints because he's dangerous
The dead man walking out of his cell was not quite sane
Lundren's wrists and ankles were securely shackled in
chains
Seth was brought into a chamber,
and sat down in the electric chair
There was a large audience that whispered,
gawked, and stared
A spectator taunted Seth in the name of all that's right
He said, "When you finally get to Hell,
don't forget to write.
I hear Hades is nice this time of year.

You'll have a chance to rest even if your ass were to sear."
The sheriff eagerly asked,
"Do you have any last words?"
Lundren swore at the elected official,
and flipped him the bird
Because Seth was strapped down to the
chair he couldn't scratch an itch
The sheriff had a smile ear to ear,
and promptly pulled the switch
If urine and blood spilled onto
the floor the janitor would mop it
Seth's eyeballs rolled to the back of his head,
and then popped out of its' sockets
The electrical current was shut off/
An examiner checked the body that was fried
Applause came from the room of spectators
because Seth Lundren had died

BEACH BLUES

What's up? Surf's up/Ship ahoy
I'm a lifeguard/Yes, the real McCoy
I've had this job for less than seven days
Don't want to work/Rather sit back and catch some rays
Watched babes in bikinis back in the day
Now I'd prefer to see them maimed from far away
Didn't give me their phone numbers, that'll make them pay
Maybe I shouldn't have kept them in the dark
These waters are inhabited by a great white shark
Everyone should know by now, I won't lift a finger to help
Stay calm, keep cool, and compose yourself
People running on the beach/More fun in the sun
The shark killed six people/Pure pandemonium
Should have put out a sign: "There's a shark, beware"
Instead I said, "Go in the water if you dare"
Suzy screamed, "Please, somebody help my boyfriend Dan!"
Too bad that I'm busy working on my tan
If I weren't preoccupied I'd do what I can
But I'm drinking a six pack because I'm the man
Suzy cried, "The shark tore Danny to pieces. Life isn't fair!"

It seems she has me confused with somebody that cares
A mother in the sand feared for the life of her daughter
Bitch shouldn't have left her alone in the water
You're welcome to bring all of your children to the slaughter
There's really only one rule you should follow:
Never bore me with your trivial requests
When it comes to saving hides I'll do my best
Run away from the beach as you cringe and cower
Because that great white is sure to devour
Anyone in the ocean/Day or night
I'll be stretched out watching with a cool Bud light

AN OLD FASHIONED HOE DOWN

Time to celebrate, boy/Go play that fiddle
No conviction for me/I received an acquittal
You should be pleased ma'am/At least just a little
Need to sit down and eat them vittles
Got a few hash browns and some baked beans
Well known for my temper/I get cranky and real mean
If Conner is on my property his life's at stake
Trespassing around here is a deadly mistake
A double barrel shotgun is all it takes
Conner lying in a coffin/Wife sobbing at the wake
Later I attacked Millie/She sprayed me with mace
Good thing I brought Bobbi Jo" just in case
That is the name of my trusty pickaxe
Hit the woman in her neck/What you think about that?
And I ain't got much edu-beh-cation
My son Ernie buried Millie with no hesitation
Boy better make sure that all the hogs are fed
People in town think we're all inbred
They rile up the family, and we get the fuss'n
Pappy married to my auntie, and my brother to a cousin
Ernie got blood stains on his overalls
I chopped up a neighbor while my daughter played with dolls

Placed pieces in a sack/Then I brought it out back
Hopped over a log/Fed the neighbor to the hogs
Now that's what I call, "real good eating"
If the sheriff comes along he's going get a beating
I'm a good farmer that's sure to feed the livestock
If the cops come I'll have to burn my marijuana crops
Just got released from prison/I don't want to get caught
There are fifteen cadavers in the barn that'll rot

BABY
FORMULA

BABY FORMULA

Cyline
Cyanide

SWEET LULLABY

Betty adopted eight children under the age of three
I'm the new babysitter on the scene
My employer had a hot date/So she dressed risqué
Should have listed "dementia" on my resume
I'm a little crazy/I don't take any crap
Melinda misbehaved and she got herself slapped
Betty left for her date/She didn't know I was capable
Of causing chaos, because I'm tough and bold
When I strangled Melinda in her sleep her body turned
cold
I was dealt a good hand in life/Never ready to fold
Stretch to stay limber/Don't want to become stiff
Pushed four little bastards off the edge of a cliff
As a babysitter I don't make enough dough
Watch them hit the jagged rocks that are down below
The mother better hurry back from her date
Or I'm afraid it'll be too late
If Zach gets thirsty he can drink some cola
While I mix cyanide in the baby's formula
Cannot teach an old dog new tricks/
Any puzzle I can decipher
Eager to pour anthrax onto the baby's diaper
Kathy died from shaken baby syndrome/
I'll make some shake n' bake

Crying far too much is all that it takes
For me to lose my cool and eventually snap
Anyway, it was time for Kathy to take a dirt nap
Now I lay me down to sleep/
I was determined to stop her heartbeat
The house became cold so I turned on the heat
I buried Janet in the playground six feet deep
Wish I could've have killed these kids all day
Going to put this baby in the microwave, yay
People accuse me of not having a soul
Guacamole and melted cheese, mixed in a bowl
Removed the infant from the appliance/Let it marinate
Allowed an hour to pass/Then I sat down and ate
Later when my employer returned she wanted to know
What happened to the children?/Where did they all go?
Betty refused to pay my babysitting fee
I used a hockey stick to shatter her knee
Then the old slut tried to limp away
I said, "It'll cost you your life ma'am/You better pay"
How could Betty do this to me?/How low can she go?
I dragged her out onto the patio
The apartment loft was on the fourth floor/Can you see?
I threw "Sweet Betty" over the balcony
I was satisfied and content with her defeat
As I watched Betty's body hit the concrete

The infant is still on the table/Haven't eaten in a while
I stared down at my dead employer,
scratched my head and smiled

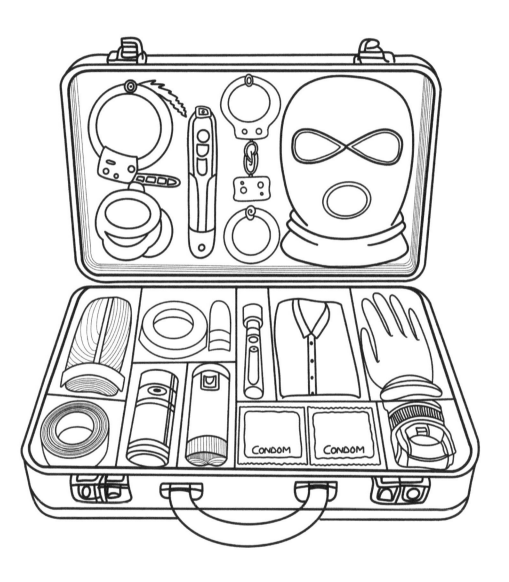

GREETINGS FROM YOUR NEIGHBORHOOD RAPIST

Ronnie has an itch that he can't seem to scratch
Found a couple late in the alley/
Chopped the boyfriend with an axe
Kidnapped the girlfriend/
Threw her in the back of his van
Beat the unsuspecting woman until she couldn't stand
When it comes to committing these vile acts,
he would never quit
Ronnie never went anywhere without a rape kit
Handcuffs, flashlight, gloves, and a ski mask
There is more/Do you really need to ask?
A change of clothes, condoms, and packing tape
This is the fifteenth victim for Heaven's sake
There were contingency disposal sites just in case
It was intended for the girl to disappear without a trace
Ronnie had nothing to lose, but much more to gain
Known as a serial rapist/The glamour and fame
After the sexual assault the poor woman was maimed
The victim didn't make it/Oh, what a shame
Ronnie thought, "That girl was a dope
With no effort to escape, didn't have to bind her with
rope"

Ronnie was pleased that there was no interruption
He got in the front seat of his van, and drove
from the place of abduction
There was no way that Ronnie could conceal his grin
He spotted a woman walking alone/Here we go again
Ronnie pulled a stocking over his head/
Got out of the van with a crowbar in hand
The woman glanced at Ronnie then she quickly ran
Ronnie thought, "I shouldn't have left the vehicle/
My judgment was erroneous
But if I run her over with the van that'll be a bonus"
The woman continued to flee on foot/
She should have watched her back
Ronnie performed a hit and run/
The victim was laced with tire tracks
There seemed to be no witnesses/Not even one sight
The man got away with murder on such a venturous
night

IT'S A SMALL WORLD AFTER ALL

We are little people four feet tall
Do not antagonize us/You will surely fall
Our outward appearance is sweet/But we are not weak
Tempers will flare and havoc we'll wreak
Alfred's verbally abusive/In his house we'll sneak
What comes next for this merry band of freaks?
Alfred was hogtied with an extension cord
We did what we wanted to our own accord
The man refused to apologize/That was his decision
A dozen of us beat Alfred into submission
Al had a punctured lung and a broken jaw
The extension cord was removed/
Then he attempted to crawl
Alfred was no longer verbally combative/
He pleaded and begged
Four little men used their mallets to break Al's legs
Was that going too far?/Were we in the wrong?
I used a pair of pliers to remove Al's tongue
Never again would he ever talk shit
A few of us found this amusing/ That I admit
For all the times we were called, "half men and gnomes"
It was appropriate for us to illegally enter Al's home

All the name calling/So pretentious and bold
Well, if we're really leprechauns then where is the gold?
We weren't exactly quiet as a mouse
Since we were already here, might as well rob the house
Got a Rolex and cash/Poor Alfred is in pain
We took stock bonds, rings, and even a gold chain
All of his appliances were going, including his stove
There was no furniture left/How's that for a gnome?
Anything not taken was simply wrecked
I felt sorry for Al and snapped his neck

LITTERBUGS BEWARE

Wendy, April, and Kubert were
environmentalists that care
They felt the destruction of wild life just isn't fair
It was their right to protest the bulldozing
of a forest preservation
They constantly did work for the environment
 all across the nation
Peter was a careless man that threw
 his garbage on the ground
One week later, all of his remains were found
An autopsy was conducted/
The cause of death was inconclusive
Kubert, Wendy, and April were all incredibly ruthless
Monique never bothered to recycle/
She thought the process was useless
April smacked her so hard in the face,
she left the woman toothless
Kubert thought the grass wasn't well kept,
which caused his blood to boil
He quickly pulled down his pants to defecate on the soil
Kubert said, "There just isn't enough manure
But that's okay because I've got the cure
I'm a vegetarian so I know the feces is pure
I have to force myself so will surely endure

49

A sore asshole and no toilet paper
Somebody went and stole mine/
That's an unsolved caper."
Denise was a woman solely concerned with her looks
She removed a hairspray container from her purse/
Of course that's all it took
April said, "Don't spray an aerosol can/Don't you care?
You're helping to destroy the ozone layer."
April struck a match and snatched
the can away with much desire
She pressed down on the nozzle and lit Denise on fire
As far as April was concerned,
Denise was pitiful and null
April felt fine about torching the woman/
Clothes and flesh are combustible
Wendy knew that anyone contributing to the
Earth's destruction shouldn't live among the human race
She spotted Gus doing so, and she shot him in the face
The activists were against litterbugs/
They were not with the times
All dead people are biodegradable/
So killing Gus was not a crime

BAG FULL OF TRICKS

Jezebels and gentlemen/Come one, come all
Quite a show is planned near the town hall
Low class citizens of all kind are welcome
Because upscale clientele make their appearance seldom
While it's still daylight they rather play cricket
That makes it more difficult to sell a significant
amount of tickets
Marley the magician loves to perform at outdoor events
It is known throughout the community that
Marley is a deviant
The magician had a show to do/With very little to say
A week ago he ditched his wife's corpse
 in the Florida Everglades
The woman was in complete contrast to
what Marley really wants
Marley killed his wife, threw her in the trunk of his car,
and drove out to the swamps
This was the kind of "disappearing act"
a few of us could appreciate
Doing such deeds left Marley famished/
He made dinner reservations and ate
Time for the show to begin/
People gathered around and stared
Marley pulled a colt .45 from his top hat and

pulled the trigger without a care
The bullet struck old Mrs. Jensen in her forehead/
It was a fatal blow
All of the present town folk applauded/
They thought it was part of the show/
Marley pulled a long scarf from his sleeve/
Louise stood too close to the stage
The magician used it to strangle Louise/
It was like putting a mouse in a lion's cage
For Marley's next trick someone must assist on his behalf
Simone promptly got on stage/
She was bound to be cut in half
The assistant lied down in a box/
Marley covered her with a cloak
He mumbled incoherent gibberish/
Then the stage was engulfed in smoke
Marley used a saw to cut through the box/
And he was well taught
Simone's cries were unbearable/That, I kid you not
Blood flooded the stage/It was a horrific scene
With the hocus pocus, Abracadabra/Everybody screamed
The two halves of the box were separated/
Simone's intestines hung out in a bunch
The magic act also revealed what Simone
had eaten for lunch
The viewing public had more than enough of

Marley's antics
Many of the attending audience
members ran away in a panic
What were Marley's motives?/If he could live with him-
self, how? The magician walked across
the stage and proudly took a bow

INDECISIVE LOVE LETTER

You are the woman of my dreams/No one can compare
I wish you cancer and death/You're my worst nightmare
I've got a gift for you, darling/Your very own mink coat
Ooh, I can't wait to get my hands around your throat
Honey, have you lost weight?/You look so thin
I'll use this aluminum bat to bash your brains in
Remember when I put the wedding band on your finger,
and you said, "I do"?
A warm sulfuric acid bath will turn your flesh into goo
I've always been a good provider/
You could never call me lazy
When I get through with you, you'll be pushing up daisies
The touch of your hand still warms my heart
One more word out of you and I'll pick your skull apart
No one can ever love you as much as I do/
That subject is not debatable
The explosive that is set underneath
your car is categorically untraceable
I could buy the kitten that you always wanted,
but then it wouldn't be a surprise
Two pit bulls, plus one rottweiler equals your demise
Let's go on a picnic, then a hot air balloon ride
It will go up in flames like the Hindenburg/
It's pure suicide

I see my soul mate when I look deep into your eyes
Put your head between your legs and kiss your ass goodbye
I can't stand to have you far from my sight
If killing you is wrong, I don't want to be right
You make the funniest remarks/
So witty and keen
Police officers will be appalled
when they arrive at the crime scene
I will always love you until my dying day
It won't be hard for me to watch as your corpse
slowly decays
I believe that you are from the heavens/
You are undeniably divine
I will cash in on your life insurance policy/
Don't worry I'll be fine
Can't wait until you're back in my arms for a hug and kiss
A sniper is stationed on the rooftop/
I hope he doesn't miss
It's unfortunate that you won't get a
 chance to read this letter/
The reason is kind of scary
I decapitated you with a meat cleaver/
Now it's time to get buried

CATERING FOR CUNTS

Chef Torry was a master of the culinary arts
One day Kayla harshly criticized his apple tart
She wrote in her column for all the world to see,
"The Chef's apple tart is fruitless and tastes like pee"
Since then, Torry's reputation had become tainted
Chef desired revenge/So he sat back and waited
Tuesday, Chef Torry invited Kayla over to his flat
Hoping for a rebuttal to be printed and frivolous chat
Kayla listened to the radio while
Torry did what he does best,
Preparing a dessert and gawking at the columnist's chest
He must add sugar/No rest for the wicked
Torry thought, "I'll serve this bitch crow,
now that's the ticket."
Chef's stirring the batter and pouring the mix
Those crunchy peanut butter cookies made Kayla sick
Chef Torry is an unbelievable prick
Rat poison was a core ingredient that gave the
cookies a little kick
Kayla was on her knees, clutching her stomach/Oh fudge
She violently vomited oodles of green blood
No more cookies for Santa, or a glass of sour milk
It is certain that Chef Torry felt absolutely no guilt
Kayla ate five cookies and gluttony is a sin

The hungry whore got what she deserved/
On Torry's face was a grin
There was left over batter, so Kayla was battered
With a wooden cricket paddle until her brain rattled
Inside of her skull that was soon to be cracked
Similar to an eggshell/ Now that's a fact
Chef Torry took a five minute break to play with his cat
After making sure that
Kayla's entrails were no longer intact
The columnist was gutted much like a fish
It was contrary to Kayla's dying wish;
To be left alone and to escape with her life
Not to have her crotch burned
with a smoldering hot pipe
Chef Torry could not stand the lies
that Kayla had spewed
The columnist was now dead for
writing a negative review

INHERITANCE REVOKED

Great Uncle Barton was on his deathbed
His nieces Sandy and Suzie stayed at his homestead
Barton was a rich eighty-eight year old
man with plenty of dough
So his spoiled middle-aged nieces couldn't
wait to see him go
Suzie and Sandy were constantly at odds with each other
over their uncle's will
If they found the terms unsuitable,
they will contest and appeal
It was just as Sandy had feared
Suzie was trying to kill her/She said,
"Have a cup of tea, dear"
The younger sister was determined
to be the only surviving heiress
She could not allow Sandy to live/
That would be far too careless
Of course Sandy was skeptical/
Suzie wanted her to drink quick
Because the hot cup of tea contained arsenic
A powerful poison compound bound to eliminate
Suzie's competition and to seal Sandy's fate
But alas, Sandy was quite clumsy and
pretended to take ill

She swung her arm at the cup/
The tea was knocked over and spilled
Suzie hastily escorted her sister over to the kitchen sink
She splashed Sandy's face with cold water/
There was little time to think
Of a contingency plan to finish off her sibling/
The sink was now full of water
Sandy was aware of her sister's wicked plan/
She forced Suzie's head down and drowned her
The older sister felt at ease/
Thanks to the "dearly departed"
No more attempts made on her life/
It was good riddance to rancid garbage
Sandy went upstairs to her great uncle's bedroom/
The old man appeared to be sleeping
The woman didn't see anyone around
so she began creeping
Sandy went inside of Barton's room/
She stood over her uncle's bed with a pillow in hand
The "faithful niece" was ready to suffocate Barton/
She reached over the nightstand
Before the murder could take place/
The bedroom closet had an opening
Sandy thought there were no witnesses/
This she was clearly hoping
A double barrel shotgun was held out from the closet/It

was aimed at the perpetrator's back
Sandy leaned over Barton with the pillow/
The shotgun was discharged next to a shoe rack
The middle-aged woman was struck with bullets/
She flopped onto the floor
Sandy now ceased living/
A man with the firearm stepped past the door
Barton sat up in his bed/
He had been awake for quite a while
The old man looked down at his
deceased great-niece and simply smiled
A servant came upstairs and
 informed Barton of Suzie's death
The butler was in hysterics/
Uncle Barton said, "My friend, do not fret
I knew what these callous cows probably had in mind
That is why I instructed my bodyguard
to go inside the closet and hide
Use any artillery necessary/
So he chose that sawed off shotgun
Blow the heads off of those two harpies/
That should be fun"
The wily old man was satisfied with current events/
He certainly did not weep
Barton ordered his servants to discard the bodies/
And now he was in for a good night sleep

MERRY MALPRACTICE

It's time to operate/This procedure is a piece of cake
For Mervin the surgeon/even though he drank burbon/
Annie was far from safe
That was his ill fated patient
Mervin had very little patience
The doctor imbibed liquor for a kick/
His procedures were quick
As a raging alcoholic, Mervin needed to get his fix
Annie required one of her kidneys to be removed
She was oblivious that this would
ultimately lead to her doom
Mervin forgot to sterilize his hands, and
 he really didn't give a damn
The doctor barely remembered to give
Annie anesthesia because he was an inebriated man
Mervin didn't wear gloves when he made an incision/
That was primarily his decision
This did not matter to the M.D. because
Annie was now under his submission
A snip here a tug there/His operating staff were fully aware
Not to challenge Mervin's authority/
The doc was belligerent and would often swear
A little nip and lots of tuck/If Annie were to survive
she required plenty of good luck

Because there was no more burbon in Mervin's Dixie cup
The good doctor was thirsty and drunk it all
This lush surgeon even had the gall
To continue the procedure just as planned
As long as Mervin is conscious he'll do what he can
To remove the patient's malignant tumor from her throat
Perhaps the surgeon should wash his hands with soap
Mervin removed Annie's tongue and her vocal chords
The doctor conducted this procedure to his own accord
One of the assistants passed out onto the floor
Mervin severed and sliced/He wanted to cut more
This is a deed the doctor shouldn't have done
Tumor in Annie's throat?/I'm afraid there was none
Mervin misread the patient's chart
No longer was there a beat from Annie's heart
The doctor will lose his medical license,
and probably do prison time
None of the other physicians were surprised
when Annie flatlined

TRASH TALK

Garbage man, garbage man,
look what I found in the garbage can
A mutilated corpse with a missing head/
Now I'll just be god damned
Garbage man, to no surprise, in the alleyway
four more bodies lie
What a sight, but at least they have their heads/
I think I'm going to cry
Garbage man, don't you see what these
cadavers mean to me?
I'm glad these people have been laid to rest/
Now their souls are truly free
Garbage man, there's so much blood/
That man over there is such a stud
Now unfortunately for him,
his body is covered in mud
Garbage man, garbage man,
the dearly departed will be sorely missed
I just sniffed a dead old lady's crotch,
and it smells like fish
Garbage man, garbage man,
guess what else is in the garbage can
An infant child that has obviously been
slaughtered like a lamb

Garbage man, I honestly think that it
came from a teenage mom
We're so close to the high school,
and last night was the prom
Garbage man, a pedestrian screamed/
I admit it's a horrific scene
Someone committed mass murder/
Or at least it seems
Garbage man, tell me why we are born just to die
Don't inform me of the afterlife,
because that's just one great lie
Garbage man, this is so sad/I want to play my violin
Instead, I will hold up my flask,
and make a toast/Then I'll sip my gin
Garbage man, there are pearls around
the neck of that dead whore
I'll take them to the nearest pawnshop/
She won't need them anymore
Garbage man, this is quite a mess/
At this profession you are best
Cleaning scum and removing filth/
Today you'll get no rest
Garbage man, please, don't sigh/
Let's get in your truck and ride
Take these bodies to the nearest landfill
if you can spare the time

Garbage man, don't call the cops/
These people's deaths were not my fault
Although the perpetrator of these
acts have yet to be caught
Garbage man, garbage man,
I'm leaving but it's been a blast
When the police arrive please inform
them to French Kiss my ass

THE RAPTURE OF ROAD RAGE

Harvey was driving home from work/Strung out in a daze
His boss let the "wild animal" loose from its cage
Harvey's temper was flaring/He was quite deranged
Perhaps it was time for a little road rage
The paralegal tried to stay calm, but he couldn't relax
Harvey ran other drivers off the road is
if he were "Mad Max"
The distraught man stopped at a traffic light
that had turned red
A senior citizen was in her car staring at Harvey with dread
Harvey glimpsed at the old shrew,
and reached underneath his seat
He pulled out a twelve gauge shotgun/
The woman was dead meat
Harvey blissfully smiled as he aimed his weapon,
and pulled the trigger
The loud blast from the firearm caused
other motorists to quiver
Children were fleeing down the street screaming in fright
An old woman's brain in her lap/Oh what a delight
Harvey sped off in his vehicle after another driver
That cut him off in traffic like an aggressive rival

The "opposition" laughed and flipped Harvey the bird
Any thought of riling this paralegal was absurd
Harvey peeled rubber/Pushing pedal to the metal
No time soon were his nerves going to settle
A postal worker crossed the street/
He was on his delivery route
Harvey ran him over/It was time for "lights out"
Blood and mail covered the windshield of his automobile
His path was obstructed/This reality was surreal
Harvey yelled, "If only I would have passed the bar
I would have my own firm by now, and a much nicer car
With no official license to practice law
I play assistant/Jumping through hoops like a dog."
The car spun out of control,
and ran through the wall of an inn
Harvey was dead at the wheel/On his face was a grin

BLOOD STONES AND RUBIES

It may drizzle but when it rains it pours
Snuffing out a young life/Another
victim breathes no more
Ruby was quite attractive and smitten with Drake
But the play boy cheated on Ruby/
His dead body was drawn from the lake
There is nothing worse than a woman scorn
When Drake's nude corpse was discovered,
his testicles were torn
Ruby danced with glee while eating cake
She had a glorious time at her ex-boyfriend's wake
Later that evening, Ruby was expecting
a gentleman caller at her home
She feverishly played the xylophone
with human femur bones
Then Ruby cracked her knuckles and
sharpened some knives
There's no such thing as taking too many lives
The doorbell rang/Ruby's date had arrived
Was this a night that Leonard had a fair chance to survive?
Probably not/Ruby invited her guest in
Oh thank God that murder is a sin

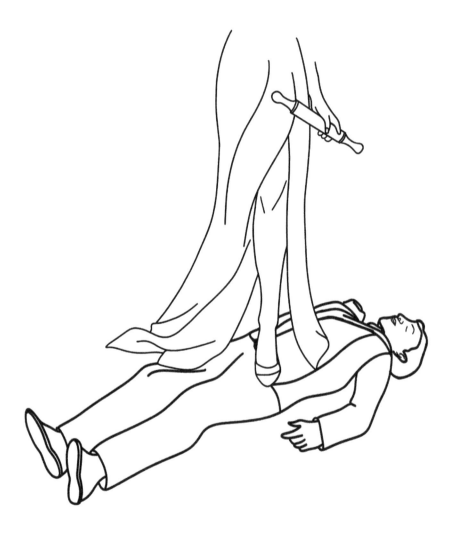

Leonard sat down on the couch and
straightened his neck tie
Ruby stood behind the insurance salesman and sighed
Lord who is in Heaven/Father be thy name
This giddy gal named Ruby was a far cry from sane
She dumped a steaming pot of mash
potatoes over Leonard's head
The gallant unsuspecting man howled in pain and fled
Ruby's resourcefulness caused Leonard
to stop dead in his tracks
The sweet, young beauty grabbed a meat cleaver,
and hit Leo in his back
Ruby could not stop smiling as her beau
crawled across the kitchen floor
The insurance man was losing blood fast/
And Ruby wanted to see more
She almost stumbled over in her high heels/
But she managed to walk correctly again
Ruby pulled a drawer open,
and with zeal picked up a rolling pin
This lady's long dress had a slit/
Ruby liked to show a little leg
She rapidly swung her rolling pin/
Beating Leonard like an egg
Blood was spattered on the wall and Ruby's pretty dress
Those stains could never be washed out,

which caused the woman distress
Leonard was no longer breathing/
But he owed money for Ruby's outfit
Leo's pocket was picked/this woman was sick/
One more victim then maybe she'll quit

SKIN TIGHT

The organ plays and the candles begin to flicker
Ken used a knife to peel off his victim's face like a sticker
Elizabeth was his beloved, closest, and dearest
Ken was always within the proximity of prostitutes/
This was curious
He had become a nobleman/The "Earl of Eerie"
Elizabeth cried out, "Please, don't come near me!"
Alas, it was too late/She didn't know what was at stake
Her life was taken by an object made of metal
She was struck in the head with a tea kettle
It was heavier than most/An old family heirloom
Sweet death couldn't come a moment too soon
Ken performed the naughty deed/
he was careful and took heed
The Earl was so much like his brother/
He placed Elizabeth with the others
Ken occupied the castle on the hillside for less than a year
A nobleman made worthy shall have no fear
Elizabeth's demise damn near brought Ken to tears
Then he came to his senses/The fresh corpse he leered
Ken removed Elizabeth's clothing/Then he began to sneer
Beth was his prize/A whore
with a reputation that had been smeared
The Earl was surrounded by

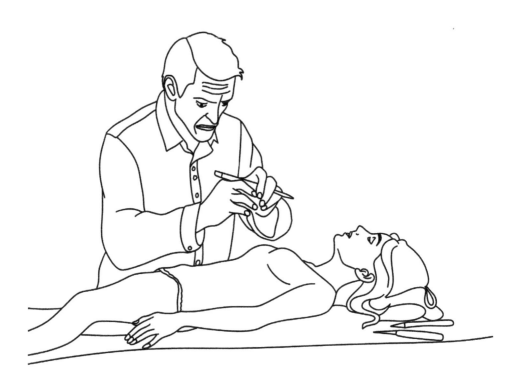

80

dead bodies stacked neatly in piles
He gently stroked the hair of his beloved/All the while
Pondering if he should do what he does best
Elizabeth should be treated properly like all of the rest
Without prejudice, the Earl killed with pride
Ken wished that Elizabeth could have been skinned alive
Tormenting his victims is an act that takes time
The Earl grabbed a knife/
He may leave on the drop of a dime
This matter was not up for discussion
If Elizabeth had only suffered a mild concussion...
But the blow was much too forceful, harsh, and fatal
The Earl of Eerie began peeling
Elizabeth's skin like a potato

GUESS WHO IS EATEN FOR DINNER

Hello, my dear/Would you like some ice cream
I'll remove the gag if you promise not to scream
Becky, you're such a sweet/
That's why I tied you to the chair
For you to escape, is a thought I cannot bear
I don't have money to buy diamond earrings,
but I brought you a severed ear
It once belonged to Melissa/Her nude carcass is near
Unfortunately, I had to teach her a lesson/Because she
wouldn't keep still
I cut her with a hacksaw,
and threw slabs of Melissa on the grill
Smell the smoke from the charcoal/
/Don't you like the aroma?
Your best friend Caroline is currently in a coma
Perhaps one day she'll wake but not before I bake
The woman's kidneys, and pound
 her brain into ground steak
I will serve fecal matter for appetizers/
Don't you dare say,
"I'm full of shit."
I'll dispose of this jezebel's remains as I see fit

Why do you look at me that way?/Please do not cry
Unless your goal is to agitate me,
because you cannot wait to die
If you smile for me,
I'll grab a hammer and break out all your teeth
Skin your worthless corpse for all that delicious meat
Stuff what's left of your body
underneath my bed for weeks
Shortly afterward,
I'll have to remove it because it'll start to reek
But that's all wishful thinking/You are safe for now
Until I become famished and
my stomach begins to growl
Should I make spaghetti out of your intestines, a
nd marinate your appendix in blood?
If you underestimate my culinary prowess,
your name will surely be Mud
There are so many delectable dishes
for me to choose from
I dissected Cody then placed his penis in a hotdog bun
You may now feel slightly out of place
A cheese grater will be used to remove your face
The magnificent seven-course meal that
I've planned for this evening is you
Dinner time has come and there is nothing you can do
I'll cook you in a human size rotisserie

located near the gallows
I will chew each mouthful of crispy
food forty times and swallow
There is a sedative I can administer that
will put you right to sleep
Your body will be coated with honey glaze/
And to me, "Bon Appetite!"

IT'S A GOOD DAY TO DIE

The coroner pulls the white sheet over dead meat
Maggots dine on decomposing bodies/Bon appetite
The cemetery lawn is freshly cut
By the grounds keeper that is stuck in a rut
He does his job well/ The cadavers will never tell
That he accommodates necrophiliacs/Love for sale
Damnation and cremation goes hand in hand
In the hourglass there are no more falling grains of sand
Burn baby burn/Your ashes in an urn
Or the flesh of rotten corpses eaten by worms
Teenagers vandalize the eternal resting place
by knocking over headstones
Then they piss on the graves, laugh, and run home
Morticians are make up artists/Talented as can be
No prosthetics are added even to an amputee
Paraplegics are energetically shoved into a box
Hauled over to the shore and thrown off of the dock
Or shredded in a wood chipper, and sprinkled over a field
Raw sliced meat from the deli that can make you ill
Think outside the box/Pick a burial plot
Lot# 273 Is the perfect spot
The funeral director set a flower arrangement/
Oh, what fun
An old lady bit the dust/Her life is done

Time to smile at the wake/Stand tall and applaud
The "old bird" is dead/Isn't that odd?
A miserable shrew and a worthless clod
She always prayed to Jesus/Now where is your God?
The end is not near/It is indeed here
All must know there's no reason to fear
Most people that die are doing what they do best
So, lie down in your coffin, close your eyes and rest

ASSISTANCE TO THE AFTERLIFE

Hi, little girl/Do you like to skip rope?
When you're done, don't hesitate to wrap
the end of it around your throat
I'll tie the other end to the ceiling fan without a care
Make sure your noose is tight, and step up on the chair
Give the noose a little tug to make sure that it's snug
I suppose you're slightly nervous/
I see a urine stain on the rug
My baked goods are on the table/
Would you like to try a muffin?
Shall we enter the kitchen?/
You can stick your head in the oven
Allow yourself to get comfortable/
Rest your weary head on the rack
I'll turn on the gas/While you go take a nap
What do you mean, "No"?/There's no need for strife
Don't you want to see your papa in the afterlife?
Why don't we go up to the roof, then stand over the edge?
Go and take a leap of faith off the building ledge
How dare you call me a liar?!/
I'll jump with you, there's no doubt
You're over exerting yourself, there's no reason to shout

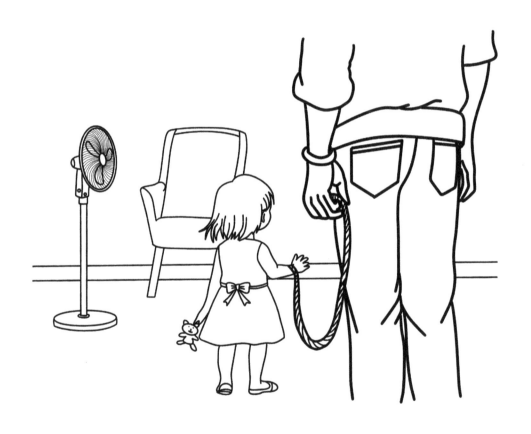

Try to calm down and relax/I'll run you a warm bath
If you fight me on this issue, you shall feel my wrath
Why not enjoy the soothing water?/
My dear, you've got it made
I will leave nearby the tub some rusty razorblades
Earlier for lunch you ate some croquette and fish/
Bare your arms and make a wish
Pick up one of those nifty razorblades,
and merrily slit your wrists
It's okay to take sleeping medication while your in the tub
You may sink down in the water going,
"blub, blub, blub, blub"
If you truly want to move forward,
we have to make you able
To have your suicide enabled/
So, please drink this liquid drano
Sweetie, you didn't finish your chores/
Must I pick up the slack?
Let's go down to the subway and catch a train/
You can wait on the track
This is going nowhere fast/Let's not play any games
I finished writing a suicide note,
and promptly signed your name
My job here is to assist you/
Girl, you should learn your place
I will place a revolver in your hand,

after I shoot you in the face
Your papa would have been pleased
to gaze upon your smiling face again
But instead, I will send you straight Hell/
You will roast in Satan's den
There is no reason to be sad/
I'll put your mind at ease
When I point this Smith and Wesson,
smile for me and say, "Cheese!"

FLY ME TO HELL

Better arrive at the airport two hours
before your departure
It is certainly worth flying all the way to Hartford
Security "gets off" while staring at your body scan
The masturbation is frequent
when holding something in their hands
Passengers are always frisked/
What do you think of this?
Security becomes aroused/
Getting cheap feels is bliss
Pay eighty dollars more just for your baggage
Give the airlines more money because they gotta have it
Flight 666 is ready to soar/All passengers are to board
Sit down and buckle your safety belts
Don't bother asking the stewardess for help
Lose weight if you're too fat/Too bad that you're obese
That is why we require you to pay for two airline seats
Bite us if you don't like our regulations
They are all the same across the nation
Sit up in your seats/Try not to slouch
Captain Flynt's flying the plane/He is certainly a grouch
That is drinking hard liquor/The amount is substantial
He boarded the plane with two bottles of Jack Daniels
Ten minutes later, the jet was in the air

The "seatbelts" sign was displayed/Get up if you dare
Two movies shown aboard the plane were terrible and dull
A passenger was pistol whipped by the air marshal
No reason for it really/The officer became bored
He spat on the injured man that fell onto the floor
Flynt became restless and knocked
his co-pilot unconscious
The captain was ready to stir up
trouble because he lacked a conscience
Flynt was drunk not a punk, surly, and all too obnoxious
This pilot flew by the seat of his pants/
Very rarely cautious
Claudia, his most loyal stewardess entered the cockpit
Flynt's feet were up over the aviation controls,
while he ate chips and dip
The captain was incapable of sitting upright/
He threw up all over the controls
Flynt turned and smiled at the stewardess/
He said, "Inform the passengers, down we go"
Claudia rushed out from the cockpit/
She didn't look back since
Suddenly the aircraft was hit with monstrous turbulence
A voice was heard over the loud speaker,
and the volume was turned up high
The captain said, "Be sure to kiss your ass goodbye
because we're all going to die!"

Many passengers began to scream/
Claudia wished it were safe by now
The aircraft's engine ceased to work/
The commotion was far too loud
People continued to panic/
There were no oxygen masks
Passengers were distraught and they could only gasp.
One man opened the emergency
exit door with nowhere to go
He took a giant leap of faith and screamed, "Geronimo!"
Life is such a funny thing/Full of twists, turns, and sins
Soon the aircraft swiftly crashed into the mountains
If I told you there is a happy ending to all of this,
I would be a liar
Flight 666 was completely demolished,
and there were no survivors

ALL HAIL PALIN

I must say hello to all of my constituents
Please forgive me if this doesn't make any sense
The doctor diagnosed me as being schizophrenic
his news is quite troubling, but maybe
he's just being a prick
They say my true identity is, Amanda Jayden
A single gal that used to ride horseback/
Such an attractive maiden
I do the work of Christ, and I moonlight for Satan
These physicians need to accept the fact that
my real name is Sarah Palin
An ex-governor of Alaska/
A job given up for soap suds
I can still see my darling children
when they drowned in the bath tub
Don't know much about the issues/
Foreign policies, what's are stance?
The public relations staff should have briefed me/
On that notion well, fat chance
It's not my fault that John and I lost the election
This country is still in a deep recession
You probably understand my reluctance to do interviews
Can't think of any supreme court cases/

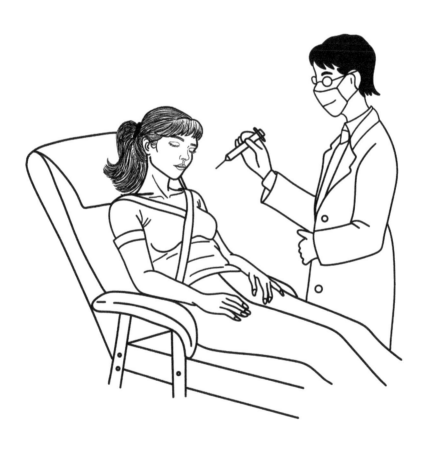

That's a fine, how do you do?
When I get frustrated murder often ensues
That bastard Levi impregnated my daughter, eww!
I neutered a stranger that looks like him/
The crime was rather grisly
His severed genitalia was tossed into the wind,
much like a Frisbee
My little girl will never know what
it's like to go to the prom
Everything I do out there is for the soccer moms
I'm not responsible for the death of my children/
Thought they were still alive
Aren't we all sick and tired of Obama's shuck and jive
Does he really think that he'll die as a martyr?/
His policies closely resemble JimmyCarter's
Don't you dare call me a bigot/You're just like all the rest
McCain and I just finished having
our Gestapo Uniforms pressed
To find out who'll be the next president
we should use a bracket
Orderly, won't you be a dear,
and help me out of this strait jacket?
I was in an automobile accident/My car is a total wreck
My baby Bristol cried herself to sleep/
Didn't mean to snap her neck

Alrighty then, I oppose abortion/
My infant child looks like an elf
If there was a chance for my mom,
she would've had one herself.

MEMOIRS OF A WHINO

Mister, can you spare some change
I was going to take a shower before you came
You're a hardworking man that needs some rest
Give me your money or I'll stab you in the chest
My cardboard sign says: I will work for food
Won't buy food but I'll gladly go and score some booze
I'm not an alcoholic/Try not to get confused
If you cannot fulfill my request you will surely lose
Your life/Such strife/Did you say that I smell?
I'll cut you, don't care if you scream or yell
Razorblades often come to my aid
This mugging is the only way that I'll ever get paid
Dear sir, won't you give me your shoes?
Your wallet or your life, which will you choose?
Bourbon on the rocks, gin and tonic, lots of rum
Jack Daniels and scotch/Wild turkey, here I come!
It's cold outside, give me your coat
Hurry before I reach for your throat
If you don't want it slit, don't have a fit
You're a big boy/You can handle it
Life sucks like lemons/We can't all be winners
It looks as though tonight you'll be paying for dinner
My favorite meal is tequila, or whiskey I think...
It's been twelve long hours since I had a drink

Giving no change often results in a penalty
My moonshine was confiscated/
They closed down the distillery
Your life will now be taken/
It's exactly as you feared
Now you know that I'll do
anything just for a glass of beer

WISHFUL THINKING

I am the magic genie of this lamp
Do not glare at me like that, you tramp
A genie can give you what ever you want
So try not to act like a stuck up cunt
It is well known that I can grant your every desire
Your neighbor is a Peeping Tom/So I will set him on fire
If that is not to your liking, may I set a bomb?
The explosion will blow your entire
block to Kingdom Come
Perhaps I'll give you an instant facelift/
You resemble Gollum from Lord Of The Rings
And you should try to lose some weight/
It wouldn't hurt to eat some lean cuisine
Do you consider my vernacular vulgar?/
It is my opinion that you look like an ogre
The drunk men in your life finally left,
because they all became sober
Is your boss at work giving you hell,
even though you accompanied him to a local motel?
He could slip on some ice and break his neck,
you tired, cheap Jezebel
Step on a crack break your mother's back
But if you spit in a stream, I'll tear out his spleen
I can never hesitate to castrate an old

reprobate and seal his fate
It is the crack of doom, and I must scratch this itch
Make a wish then we'll talk, bitch
About granting power, fame, and making you rich
They'll find your employer's dead
carcass in a roadside ditch
Why can't you get it through your head?
The world can be yours, and your enemies dead
Sue tried to steal your job with no procrastination
Her nipples can be torn off with pliers/
There will be a subsequent decapitation
The appreciation for my suggestions are quite dubious
If you don't soon make a wish I shall become furious
On second thought don't make any wishes/
This will probable become a disaster
You will have an aneurysm/Your blood vessels will pop/
I will have a new master

BANJO JIBBERISH JAM

Hey Ma, hey Pa, hey Rudy, hey Paul
I got a little song to sing for y'all
Can't stand life filled with so much strife
Should've known by now that I hate my wife
She's always inclined to hit me in the head with a skillet
Did it three more times to make sure that I feel it
Opened up a drawer, quickly grabbed my .22
Lodged a bullet in the face of Betty Sue
Danced around merrily, acting like a fool
Have blood on my hands/What am I to do?
Had to kill the winch/The bitch was getting meaner
Unfortunately, murder is more than just a misdemeanor
I'm fine, won't wine, though I don't have a dime
Like to play my harmonica and I'm drinking moonshine
Getting liquored up/Can't read between the lines
Homicide is on the rise/It's a sign of the times
Let's eat blueberry pie/My speech is slurred
The line between right and wrong has been blurred
If can't under stitch what I say/
Rotten dirt...what a bad day
My soul is damned, won't you please pray?
I was eating frog legs when I had Shirley pegged
She saw me with the corpse/

The woman pleaded and begged
Shirley was going to get away,
but you know I won't have it
I can only thank God that he granted me with a hatchet
Always sharpen the tool/I'll never let it get dull
I deeply embedded the blade of the hatchet into her skull
Two deaths in one day, what can I say?
I've been a busy beaver just hacking away
At the limbs of my victims/It's so simple
To discard the remains/I'm energetic and nimble
I can do a split like I split Shirley's head
And I thank my lucky stars that Betty Sue is dead
I'll grind them to bits, then mix them with my grits
That is their destiny that seems well fit
For real, what a deal, Betty Sue's fate is sealed
I'm so glad Shirley could also be a part of this meal
If a man is true he does what he has to do
You should all come over here and eat my stew

LAY ME DOWN TO SLEEP

Finally, I am deceased/My soul will never be at peace
If I'm placed into a cheap pine box,
the maggots will surely feast
A cold cadaver on the slab/Today rejoice/Do not be sad
Soon they will read the will/
You'll inherit everything I have
How did I die?/I'm inclined to ask
As I lie here with by big toe tagged
I've had a life that I no longer own/
The mortuary is my new home
With all the other corpses that are lying about
I shall never be alone
I just remembered taking a flying leap
Off the top of a building/
That's why I'm under this white sheet
You should've seen it/ Such an amazing feat
Hitting the concrete/brain spilled out onto the street
Time of death was 10:06 a.m./
If I had the chance I'd do it again
The seventh circle of Hell is probably where
I'll go because suicide is a sin
But the experience was so exhilarating/
To take a swan dive without hesitating

My body has been promptly delivered/
The mortician has been eagerly waiting
Arrangements have yet to be made/
An all expense funeral, what do you say?
It will be an unforgettable extravaganza/
The main event of the day
This is more than most can muster
At the wake don't forget to tip the ushers
During the vigil there will be refreshments
and chocolate cake
So much it'll give you a tummy ache
Do the Macarena and the Electric Slide
Once the jubilation has commenced/
They'll be glad I died
Soon I will be in the ground to rot
Please hurry and cover my burial plot
My body remains still and my eyes shut tight
A bloody carcass disposed of and to all a goodnight

A FIENDISH FAIRYTALE

Alright children, it's time for bed
I know this is the point of the evening that you dread
Tuck yourselves in and I'll tell you a tale of woe,
Sorrow, and pain from a long time ago
There was once a noble knight named, Sir Ben
The young man was inclined to court the
king's daughter, Princess Gwen
A cheap little harlot that's always willing and able
To sleep with all twelve knights from the roundtable
She once had a liaison with the royal jester
The king did not approve/His anger began to fester
He swiftly ordered "the fool"
to be thrown into the dungeon
Who else is to blame? There's no one else other than
Princess Gwen that's now safe and sound
The jester's hands were tightly bound
Behind his back as he was dragged up the stairs
No longer imprisoned because life isn't fair
King Ford had a change of heart/
That is usually hard to tell apart
From any other man of his position/
Should've revealed this from the very start
The jester arrived at the platform with his pride intact

He was forced to greet a masked
man that carried an axe
Royal guards forced the jester to
kneel down and atone for his crimes
Decapitation was the most
expedient solution for the times
Princess Gwen was made a fool of/
King Ford will not have it
The executioner gleefully swung his axe/
The jester's head fell into a basket
A pool of blood stained the floor/What was next in store
For a ruthless tyrant that calls himself king,
and his daughter a filthy whore?
Soon Sir Ben had heard the news
Of the Jester's sudden demise/What was he to do?
A whimsical notion came to mind/
Sir Ben leaped up from a bench
He was more determined than ever to marry the wench
Let the music play/Sound the trumpets
King Ford allowed the wedding to take place between
Sir Ben and the strumpet
After the ceremony Sir Ben was disgraced
No one could keep the princess in her place
An hour later, adultery had been committed/
Oh, what a waste

On their wedding night,
Sir Ben placed a pillow over Gwen's face
It wasn't necessary for the princess
to disappear without a trace
But he dismembered the corpse and discarded it in case
King Ford were to become
suspicious and formally announce
That Sir Ben no longer had scruples not even an ounce
The noble knight did not wish to accept the blame
If Gwen's remains are discovered and
her body found maimed
Sir Ben decided to prepare a drink for the king
While the royal entertainers were to dance and sing
The sovereign's chalice was filled wine and a toxin
Abortion of this plan cannot be an option
His royal highness was quite comfortable/
The seat of the throne is plush and soft
King Ford shouldn't have given
the poison tasters the day off
He began to have spasms and foam at the mouth
Royal subjects in the courtyard were
bewildered and they started to shout
The king stood up from the throne,
and stumbled onto the floor
Sir Ben thought his royal highness was becoming a bore

At last the sovereign had taken his final breath
The young knight was pleased about King Ford's death
He giggled uncontrollably and danced a jig
Then he urinated on his highness, and called him a fat pig
As if Sir Ben's behavior wasn't odd enough,
he began to take a horse stance
With his weapon of choice he proceeded to sodomize
the dead man with his lance
Children, I'm afraid that's all there is to tell
You're a little to young to hear the culmination of this tale
All you need to know is that Sir Ben scratched
the king like an irritating itch
Ford is dead, so is Princess Gwen/
That promiscuous little bitch
Close your eyes my little darlings/
Count severed heads not sheep
Into Slumberland you go/Have a goodnight sleep

RESTAURANT RETRIBUTION

Hello, Winston family/The other waiter had to leave,
now I'll wait on you
I snapped his neck back in the kitchen/
Well, what can you do?
You ordered a bottle of chardonnay,
tenderloin steak, and bisque
With croquette fish/ Now listen to this
We have much better bottles on our wine list/
Contradict me and I'll get pissed
Oh dear, this is no fun/I'll pull out my gun
Don't even think of attempting to run
What are Tuesday's specials, you ask?/
Quite the conundrum
I'm afraid I don't know/Perhaps there are none
But if there are you'll be the first to know
Should have ordered rice and duck with sausage gumbo
Last time you caused me to be reprimanded,
and you reap what you sow
You reported me to upper management for misconduct/
Now that was just low
I brought what you ordered with
complimentary hominy grits

Start eating, my trigger finger is beginning to itch
My sub sized pistol is well hidden
behind this menu that I hold
That day I remembered you complained
about the food being cold
Told me to take it back, and you wouldn't pay jack
For hard toasted rice, squab, and an over cooked rack
Of lamb/Hot damn!/Mix in a little spam
Add parsley and cloves/It'll still taste like sand
If you think this food is terrible, it's okay/I'm not mad
You are pleased that I'm here/That makes me glad
You're all eating now/Hope you are enjoying your food
I brought it out quickly, and you don't want to be rude
They fired me a week ago, but I shall do whatever I please
Do me a favor and hand over your car keys
I'm not a disgrace, but the grits were laced
With an undetectable, powerful, poisonous powder base
You will be incapacitated for a few minutes,
but while you're still able
Give me your wallet before you all keel over at the table
This is no joke/You will die/And there's no time for quips
I'm leaving this time with a Mercedes and a really big tip

MY BURNING LOVE

My dear Darleen asked me for a divorce
As she rides pristine on that high horse
I always knew what her true intentions were,
despite that I answered, "Of course."
Darleen was like a greedy vulture from
an egg that just hatched
I doused her with alcohol and struck a match
She wanted all of my money which
I thought was kind of funny
A conniving, duplicitous, insidious
shrew that was also cunning
But I'll have the last laugh/I didn't even have to use gas
Merely a bottle of the cheapest booze/
Unleaded is too good for her ass
I threw that match and Darleen twisted and turned
She screamed in agony as I watched her burn
The fire engulfed her entire being/
It was really quite the scene
Couldn't help but to point, laugh, and make fun/
I really shouldn't be so mean
Then again, perhaps I should go out into the backyard
and gather some wood
Throw her on top and add lighter

fluid because she is no good
My lady looked exquisite in that bright orange dress
Oh wait, those are the flames/Darleen is a disheveled mess
She seemed to have become bitter/
Her screams were now high pitched
Burn baby burn, you sassy belligerent bitch
You'd never be able to steal my fortune/
On that you can be certain
Listen to me while I'm talking to you,
and stay away from the curtains
Even if you are dazed, I don't care if you're in a haze
Watch where you are going before you set
the entire house ablaze
Darlene finally collapsed onto the floor,
and I would've been quite sore
If she had ruined any of the furniture/
That nefarious two-bit whore
I used buckets of water to extinguish the flames
Which exposed the charcoaled corpse of that wicked dame
You danced beautifully, my dear/
And you shall never be alone
After I clean up this mess and gather your bones
You'll be stuffed into some plastic
bags and buried out back
Next to the shoe box that contains your dead pet cat

My soul will always burn for you, but you burned literally
It is obvious how much I love you/Can't you see?
You know I'm just kidding, right?/
But you'll always be my girl
Nothing more than a crispy
cadaver that is no longer in this world

A JIGSAW DATE

I must apologize for my neighbors making so much racket
You didn't expect to wake up, seated at a table in my attic
Now that you're all tied up we can play a game
I'll be the killer/You are my victim to maim
If you're hungry then eat/After all, I promised you dinner
Won't live long afterward/I'm afraid
we all can't be winners
I'm not going to let you starve until you rot
I'll serve you some delicious soup that's nice and hot
Like a flame that attracts a moth/
Formaldehyde is the broth
Even if you do not gulp and simply sip
You can say goodbye to your lips,
The bottom half of your face, and your teeth
I care because you'll always be mine to keep
Just like that 14 karat gold heart shaped locket
I'll tear your arms right out of their sockets
I can use them with glee to play the bongos
Then remove the upper side of your face/I got your nose
Well, oh well... that's the way it goes
This meat cleaver is perfect to sever your toes
Must make haste/Chop, chop/No pun intended
Everyone knows that I'm sick and demented

You have a wonderful figure,
although now you're disfigured
Thank goodness there's only your legs to dismember
Hope you don't mind that
I placed my tool chest in your lap
I'll use this clamp to twist your head off like a bottle cap
My dear, you seem anxious/Please do not quiver
I'll skip rope with your intestines and fondle the liver,
Remove the kidneys and spleen/Stick them up your anus
These moments are precious to us/I'll caress your uterus
I wanted to cook a fine meal/Didn't want it to be lame
The pancreas will go well with mash potatoes and brains
You've been through a lot, but try not to be sad
I'll prepare for you a warm, soothing acid bath
After I've had my fun because it wouldn't make any sense
Not to dissolve your bones,
and clean up all traces of evidence
It has to seem as though you were never here
Try not to take it personally, my dear
On second thought, I changed my mind/
I want to be with you until the end
In fact, I can't wait to put you back together again

Sean Seville is an author/entertainer from Chicago, Illinois.

9 798893 244731